Dominic Salles still lives in Swindon, with his workaholic wife Deirdre. His jiu-jitsu-loving ex-engineer son, Harry, has moved to Shoreditch and lives on the site of Shakespeare's first theatre. Destiny. For those of you who remember Bob, he is now an ex-dog. It's curtains for Bob and The Curtain for Harry.

His daughter Jess is moving to New Zealand where the surf is better, and the rugby is better than Wales. He spent three months in Andorra this year, learning to snowboard. He is not as cool as he thinks, but he will spend part of the summer in New Zealand snowboarding on a volcano.

His sister Jacey is an actress, famous for her Spanish accent, on your TV screens in shows like Casualty and Cold Feet. She would be hilarious in her own YouTube channel. Tweet her to let her know.

His YouTube channel, Mr Salles Teaches English, has reached 100,000 subscribers, about which he is childishly excited. 30% of his viewers said they improved by at least 3 grades in 2022.

He drives a Toyota Prius and is getting solar panels this year to offset his enormous carbon footprint. I don't expect they will fit on the car though.

Other Grade 9 Guides by Mr Salles

Language

The Mr Salles Guide to **100% at AQA GCSE English Language**
The Mr Salles Guide to **Awesome Story Writing**
The Mr Salles Quick Guide to **Awesome Description**
The Mr Salles **Ultimate Guide to Description**
The Mr Salles Quick **Guide to Grammar, Punctuation and Spelling**
The Mr Salles **Ultimate Guide to Persuasive Writing**
The Mr Salles Guide to 100% in AQA GCSE **English Language Paper 1 Question 2**
The Mr Salles Guide to 100% in AQA GCSE **English Language Paper 1 Question 3**
The Mr Salles Guide to 100% in AQA GCSE **English Language Paper 1 Question 4**
The Mr Salles Guide to 100% in AQA GCSE **English Language Paper 1 Question 5**
The Mr Salles Guide to 100% in AQA GCSE **English Language Paper 2 Question 2**

Literature

The Mr Salles Guide to **GCSE English Literature**
Study Guide Mr Salles Analyses **Jekyll and Hyde**
The Mr Salles Ultimate Guide to **Macbeth**
The Mr Salles Guide to **An Inspector Calls**
The Mr Salles Ultimate Guide to **A Christmas Carol**
The Mr Salles Ultimate Guide to **Romeo and Juliet**
Mr Salles **Power and Conflict** Top Grade Essay Guide (AQA Anthology): 11 Grade 9 Exam Essays!

Books on Teaching

The Full English: How to be a brilliant English teacher
The Slightly Awesome Teacher: Using Edu-research to get brilliant results
The Unofficial Ofsted Survival Guide
Differentiate Your School: where every student learns more

Contents

What Makes a Great Story?

Ok, I'm just going to assume that you know how to write in sentences.

That's all you need to know to write the words for a short story. But that isn't the secret.

Before this, I've published two books to show you what great short stories look like. The Ultimate Guide to Short Story Writing included over 20 stories, showing what excellent 500-700 stories look like, and how to write these in a number of different genres and styles.

The Ultimate Guide to Paper 1 Question 5 shows over 20 stories from students, with several at each grade. They are all based on what students can write under exam conditions. This helps you grade your own stories and understand how to improve them.

This is the secret I haven't yet taught.

How do You Structure Your Story?

This book helps you think like a writer.

In school, we tend to practise lots of language techniques: metaphor, simile, personification, alliteration, and so on. We tell you to vary the length of your sentences, and have one sentence paragraphs, etc. We ask you to vary your punctuation (ooh! What, now? I see...)

But we spend too little time thinking about how to start the story so the reader is hooked. Or how to end it so that the reader revisits what happened and sees it in a new light. Or which perspective to tell the story from so that it is most fun to read or to make it really memorable.

So this book focuses on how to start and end your story, and how to tell it.

The Sequence of a Story Structure

1: Who Is the Character of Your Story?

2: What Do They Want?

3: Why Can't They Have What They Want?

4: What's at Stake if They Don't Get What They Want?

5: Who or What Helps Them Get What They Want?

6: How Do They Finally Get What They Want?

7: How Is the Character Transformed?

You will see how all 20 stories follow this structure.

1. How do you choose how to start?

2. How do you choose how to end?

3. Whose point of view will you tell the story from?

When you play around with your answer to those 3 questions, you will learn how to really enjoy story writing.

How to Find Story Ideas

Many students have started to copy parts of the descriptions in my guides and videos instead of thinking for themselves.

This presents two real problems. First, the examiners are starting to get to know my stuff, and so they recognise this as plagiarism and award a lower mark. Secondly, I'm not showing you that writing short stories is just great fun and a skill for life.

You can copy the plots of these stories – that is not plagiarism.

You'll never regret writing a short story, which will stay with you for life. But you'll never remember a description you copied, or even wrote for yourself. You'll never say, "I'm so lucky I took English language GCSE and practised all those description questions".

But I predict you will remember this book and, I hope, be grateful that you used it for English GCSE.

This is How the Book Works

1. Read 20 plots of 20 stories. Most of them are mostly true!
2. Find some plots you like.
3. Choose your favourite plot to practise with.
4. Pick 2 of the different ways I suggest to start the story and write them – which works best?
5. Do the same for 2 of the alternative endings I suggest – which makes the story most memorable?
6. Write the story – it will be at least grade 7. I guarantee it.
7. Give it to your teacher and ask for 5 specific changes you could make to get to grade 8 or 9, or beyond.
8. Look at 5 past papers and work out how that story could be adapted to every single question.
9. Try it again with a second story, because now you are curious to see if you can write a better story as a first draft.
10. Send them to me to make a video, or publish in my next book of short stories!

The Croc and Bull Story

Park Rangers in Kruger National Park need to sedate a bull elephant, Napoleon. They're going to put a GPS collar on him, so they can track him and improve his habitat and chances of survival. He only comes to the National park once a year, in mating season, so they must do it now. They find him with Binti, an eligible female elephant on heat, who is also pursued by a number of younger males.

They tranquilize him but it takes about half an hour to take effect. Binti is disappointed at Napoleon's decreasing effort, and starts to approach the younger elephants who are not drugged, and so the bull elephant, Napoleon, starts to chase her. She escapes across the river. But as he follows her into the middle, he suddenly becomes unconscious, slumps in the water and starts to drown. It's a crocodile infested river.

But the young ranger Rommel weighs up the risk to his life compared to losing the prize elephant. He wades in and manages to hold Napoleon's trunk above his shoulders. Each brush of fish against his legs, terrifies him as though it's the scales of a crocodile coming to attack. His shoulders burn for 20 minutes as he holds the trunk above his head, scanning the water for crocodiles. Then the giant ears flap and he knows he must run. He turns towards the shore where two crocodiles stand looking at him. Rommel freezes.

How to End the Story

1. You could end it there, and we have to imagine how he might survive.
2. Or the bull elephant could grab him with his trunk and throw him over his back, landing in the river behind, miraculously on the opposite side to the crocodiles.
3. Or the bull elephant could deliberately choose to save him, and place him on his back.

Where to Start the Story

1. In media res, shooting the tranquiliser into the elephant.
2. As a chase, following the elephant once he has been shot, while the elephant is still pursuing the mate.
3. In the water, with Rommel wondering how the hell he ended up in a crocodile infested river holding up the trunk of an enormous and dangerous bull elephant in mating season. The story is told in flashback.

Example Story Openings

1. **In Media Res**

Rommel peered through the sight, the X shape cross hairs caressing Napoleon's neck. He squinted, ignoring the heat. Patience. Breathe. Let the stillness come. Now, it had to be now. But as his trigger finger squeezed, Rommel jerked forward, driven by primal desire.

The dart sank into Napoleon's neck, just inches shy of the vein. The great bull elephant trumpeted, his ears flapped wildly and he strode towards Josephine, the latest female in season. No male dared challenge Napoleon in full flow, and indeed no female could resist his alpha status. But the mating ritual demanded a chase, and Josephine, as the rangers called her, would make Napoleon work for an heir. She would make him run.

Rommel stowed the rifle in the jeep. Amardi took the wheel, and they followed the two would be lovers at a cautious pace. The tranquiliser would take longer, having missed its mark, and Napoleon could flip the jeep like a steak on a barbecue.

2. **Chase**

Rommel sprinted for the jeep. Never, but never, cross a mating bull elephant. He'd just shot a dart into the neck of Napoleon, the most powerful Elephant in Kruger park. The intelligent, monstrous eye swivelled to him, eighty meters away, and stared at him with rage and calculation. Fifty-fifty chance of him charging, thought Rommel, and he began signalling for Amardi to start the jeep and be prepared to flee.

Suddenly, Napoleon's trunk snaked downwind – thank God. He had caught Josephine's scent. She was in season, her musk caressing the trunk's nerve endings, inflaming then with desire and the promise of an heir. Lust trumped anger. Rommel and Amardi were safe. For now.

3. **In the Water**

'Sh*t, sh*t, sh*t, sh*t,' Rommel swore at himself. His shoulders burned as he struggled to hold the great trunk out of the water. If he weakened, the great bull elephant would drown. He cursed the pain and cursed his own stupidity. He had fired just too early, the dart missing the vein, and Napoleon had sprinted away. An easy tagging had turned into a nightmare.

And this wasn't the worst part. Fear taunted him. Every fish which grazed past his bare calves in the river might have been a crocodile. Two of them eyed him from the bank, their prehistoric malevolence matched only by patience. They wouldn't risk an attack on Napoleon, the only creature on God's earth large enough to inspire fear. But Napoleon would come round soon. Josephine's musk still hung in the air, and the nerve ending's in Napoleon's trunk would light up like invisible fireworks, luring the great bull elephant with a siren song of desire.

What then? Napoleon would crush him, or spear him through with the ivory stakes of his tusks. Or, a miracle might happen – Napoleon might brush him off like an ant, too small to bother with. That left the crocodiles. They had queued patiently, like diners at an all you can eat buffet. But as soon as his sleeping minder left him, Rommel would have seconds to live. They would torpedo towards him and tear his body apart as they fought for the largest portion.

The rifle!

He called for Amardi. Amardi had the rifle. But the gun held only tranquilisers, not bullets. Better than nothing. But Amardi had never fired a rifle.

Another surge of fear swept through him.

Rommel plunged his head under, the river washing away the sweat from his eyes, calming his panicked thoughts.

What Rules You Can Learn From This?
1. Writing from the point of view of a character always works.
2. Starting with a moment of crisis always hooks the reader.
3. Introduce the backstory in one or two sentences.
4. Structure the writing around the character's thoughts and feelings, not just the events.
5. The structure is more entertaining if the character thinks about possible endings.
6. When you write three alternatives, the one you most commonly like best is the third.

Why Don't I Give These Examples for All the Stories?
1. You will learn best by doing.
2. If you just want to read great stories, you know I have already written two guides like that.
3. Writing is a form of play – like a video game, you keep playing at it to work out the hidden rules.
4. These rules 6 rules are the ones you need to level up. The only way is to play.
5. I think it is more fun that way, too!

The Problem Turkeys of Schleswig Cathedral

Lothar is a brilliant, but penniless painter. One day, his luck changes. He meets Ernst Fey, a famous art historian and painter, who offers him a job restoring damaged paintings in a famous medieval cathedral.

But these paintings are so damaged, that when Lothar touches them with his brush, the old paint turns to dust and brushes right off the plaster. So Lothar completely repaints them and once unveiled they are treated as a masterpiece. Ernst is treated as a genius. However, the restoration is a fake, containing pictures of people Lothar loves. And eight turkeys. Turkeys were not brought to Europe until Columbus, but the paintings are supposed to be from a hundred years before Columbus was born. They are an obvious fraud. No one notices.

Ernst sacks him. Lothar remains penniless while the professor is lauded as a genius. Then the turkeys are spotted. Proof of fraud? No. The paintings appear on postcards and stamps and tourists flock to the miracle in the cathedral that proves one of their countrymen discovered America 100 years before Columbus did.

Unable to bear the injustice, Lothar finally goes to the police. They arrest him and put him on trial for slandering Ernst, a national hero. He is sent to a mental asylum until he confesses that he made it all up out of jealousy, and that the pictures are real.

Where to Start the Story

1. Chronologically – the first crisis Lothar as a starving artist, wondering whether he should give up art, when he is suddenly hired by Ernst.
2. Start at the end – Lothar is weighing up whether to tell the truth, and stay in the asylum, or earn his freedom by lying. We find out the rest in flashback.
3. Start with a crisis – the paint brushing off the plaster, or the moment he is arrested.

How to End the Story

1. Lothar is sent to the mental asylum.
2. Lothar "confessing" that he made it all up.
3. Lothar, now released from the asylum, paints 8 giant turkeys over the walls of Ernst's house.

Ancestry

Erin is an only child. Luckily the Hosseinis, an Iranian family, lived next door. They had 4 children, and together with them, she would make 5. Her childhood summers were full of adventures with the children, and many an evening the two families shared meals and drinks. She was 13 when Darius's father died, and the children became even closer.

At 18, Erin realises she has always been in love with Darius, the 18 year old boy next door. At a sixth form party, celebrating their A level results and university places, she kisses Darius and discovers he feels the same way. She tells her mother Maria who, instead of talking through her feelings, simply forbids Erin to date Darius. Erin is confused. She tries to talk to her father, Declan, but he simply looks sad, and, as always, backs up Maria no matter what.

But this feels like a forbidden love, which makes it even more exciting, and her mother's unexpected reaction makes the relationship even more attractive. Darius and Erin see each other in secret, for a few short weeks, until they go to separate universities.

They are both astonished to find their love survives. They each meet exciting new people, but none make them as happy as each other. Erin decides she must tell her parents. But before she goes home, she receives a phone call. Her father has died of a heart attack.

At the funeral, no one from her father's Irish side of the family turns up. His parents are dead. There are no brothers and sisters. She makes two decisions at the end of that year. The first is to get pregnant. The second is to take a DNA test to see if she can trace her father's roots.

Darius is thrilled. He knows the value of a real father, having lost his so young, and he is determined to be a brilliant parent. Erin and Darius get the family together, to announce their news. Safety in numbers, thinks Erin.

They sit down at the dining room table, ready to tell the family, when Erin's phone pings. She glances at it and decides to open the message, as it is the result of her DNA test. She had expected to be part Irish. But there is no Irish DNA! Instead, half her DNA was Persian.

How to End the Story

1. She hands the phone to her mother, and they look at each other in horror.
2. Or, she looks down at her baby swelling in the womb in horror.
3. Or she reads the results out to everyone at the table.
4. Or she decides to say nothing.

Where to Start the Story

1. The first kiss – in media res.
2. The funeral, with a flashback to the memory of Darius's father's funeral.
3. The moment she and Darius discover Erin is pregnant.
4. Maria, seen through Erin's eyes, as she takes in what the DNA means.

I Love You

A husband receives a text from his wife's phone. It says, "I'm listening to our song. I love you Robert. I can't wait to see you tonight. XXX"

His wife Julia is away for the weekend, visiting a friend, Matilda, from her university days. He and his wife don't have a song. It is a great joke between them that he has no musical taste at all. These are both clues that the text isn't meant for him. But the biggest clue is that his name is David.

He's working late, finishing an important acquisition of a company, and he's the chief legal officer. His junior, Rebecca, is working with him. They've fancied each other for ages, but vows are vows, thinks David. He's always been professional, despite her perfume, her intelligence, her smile and laughter and the way her business clothes seem designed to remind him of her figure. They've flirted with each other before, especially at after dinner drinks. But that's where they've drawn a line.

He and Rebecca go for a drink. They flirt, and the line become blurred. He can't believe his wife is having an affair. He's hurt, and tempted, and in another life, Rebecca would be perfect. They go back to her flat for the first time.

Matilda sends him a text. She has just discovered her teenage daughters have used Julia's phone to send him a prank text.

How to End the Story

1. He receives the text the next day, as he wakes in Rebecca's bed.
2. He receives the text as he enters the room, and we end, not knowing if he will go through with it.
3. He receives the text, and goes through with it anyway.

How to Start the Story

1. With the text.
2. David and Rebecca, obviously getting along as they work hard closing the documentation. We sense their mutual attraction. Then the text arrives.
3. Mid kiss in Rebecca's flat, as we revisit everything in flashback, while the two move closer to the bed, flipping between the flashback and the present, giving David multiple chances to not take the next step.

Vomit and the Viking

Anna loves to party, who doesn't? She's doing A levels. One Saturday, she goes to a house party. It's being given by one of the cool girls, Saskia, who is clever, beautiful and rich. But once she gets to the party, there is only one thing Anna wants more than to impress Saskia, and that is to hook up with Sven, the tall, blonde Viking type, brilliant smile, blue eyes, sculpted muscles, cool fashion sense. He doesn't go to their sixth from college. He's a friend of Saskia's from who knows where.

Anna tries everything, tossing her hair, laughing ostentatiously, making eye contact across the room, then trying to talk to him. But Sven has no chat and doesn't take any of her hints. Anna drinks more and more, and though she flirts with other boys, none of them look half as exotic as Sven. Eventually, the party ends, and they all find different spots in different rooms. Sven and a few of her friends sleep in her room. They lie next to each other, their bodies inches apart, and absolutely nothing happens. Until 5 am, that is, when Anna vomits all over her own legs and, of course, on the still sleeping Sven.

Anna, embarrassed and disgusted, flees the house. She texts Saskia to tell her how disgusting Sven was, that he had puked all over her, and then just gone back to sleep. Saskia and Anna bond in mutual disgust.

That night, she texts her best friend, Marcia, and tells her what really happened. She presses send, only to find that she has sent the text to Saskia by mistake.

Where to Start the Story

1. Write the whole thing as a text – Anna retelling everything to Marcia, then realising her mistake when she presses send.
2. Write in the third person, starting at the beginning.
3. Start at the crisis – Anna seeing Sven, flirting with him and making no progress.
4. Start with anti-climax – they both settle side by side in the bedroom, but nothing happens. The rest is told in flashback as and after she vomits.

How to End the Story

1. The realisation that the text has gone to Saskia and not Marcia.
2. We find out that Sven is telling the story – perhaps to his kids – 'and that's how I met your mother'.

Rake's Progress

Amelia is fed up with her husband Tom leaving things about the house. It's never as tidy as she would like. Tom works from home while she has a 9-to-5 job, so he should make the time to keep the house tidy.

The winter nights are getting dark. The lightbulb at the back of the house goes out and Tim trips over obstacles on the path: a bucket which fills up with rainwater, a birdfeeder, a rake. As he walks back into the house from his shed, he keeps getting soaked or stumbles, or the rake smacks him in the face. He doesn't remember seeing them when he went out in the morning.

Tom resolves to fix the light. He does so, in a howling gale, and then retreats to write in his shed. Later, he hears his wife's car arrive home for the evening. He walks back to the house. But the light is off. He is furious that he hasn't fixed it properly and doesn't notice the rake. It smacks him in the face. He comes in cursing and complaining about his day and asks if his wife has turned the light off.

'Of course not.' she replies.

He hits the switch and it turns on.

'Do you know I've been smacked in the face twice with a rake today?' he asks.

'Really,' she says, 'no welcome home. How has your day been?'

But when Amelia turns away, Tom notices a huge smile spread across her face.

How to Start the Story

1. Amelia leaves in the morning, frustrated at clearing up Tom's clothes from last night, and his breakfast things for this morning.
2. Or, Tom comes downstairs and decides the washing up can wait, making his way to write in his shed.
3. Or Tom stumbles towards the light, dodging obstacles, and getting smacked in the face as he steps on the rake.
4. Or, in the middle of the storm, in media res, Tom is fixing the light. His face hurts, and we hear about his day in flashback.

How to End the Story

1. I can't think of a better way than the last line!
2. Tom sets up a camera, only to find that it is his son, or his next door neighbour.

A Good Yarn

Back when Shakespeare was a boy, wool was the most precious commodity in the country. Wool farmers grew rich and the poor were sometimes tempted to steal sheep. His father John told him this story by the kitchen fire.

So the wool farmers got together and employed a hangman, who lived down in a cottage, deep in the valley. At the top of the valley was a crossroads where four wool farms met. There the four farmers built a gibbet, and there the hangman would hang any sheep rustlers.

One stormy night, the winds were wild, and the hangman was awoken by a pounding on his door. The farmers summoned him up the hill to the crossroads, where a young boy knelt sobbing on his knees. The hangman heard only the wind, and ignored the boy's cries. Stealing was stealing, and hanging was quick, if it was done well.

And so the hooded boy was lifted high on the hangman's shoulders. He held the boy's kicking legs and expertly applied the noose. The boy was dropped, and his screams were silenced, and his legs kicked and thrashed in the air, and then he was still. The hangman pulled off the boy's hood, so that his family and friends would be warned about what happens to thieves.

At that moment, the storm blew clouds away from the full moon, to reveal the face of his son. He went down to his cottage without speaking a word. There was a hook on the kitchen wall. The hangman strung himself up on the hook with the memory of his dead boy's face contorted in the moonlight.

For decades, no one would buy the cottage. 'But that', said John, looking up at the kitchen wall, 'is why the house was so cheap, and that is why the hook hangs there still.'

How to Start the Story

1. In media res, in the storm, with the hangman being summoned
2. In the kitchen, William sitting with John by the kitchen fire

How to End the Story

1. With the hook on which the hangman hung himself
2. With John's words
3. With the gibbet, still hanging in the wind at the crossroads

Sisterhood

Jeremy Clarkson writes a hate filled article about Meghan Markle, accusing her of being a traitor and a gold digger and a manipulative woman who deserves to be paraded through the streets naked while Londoners pelt her with excrement.

This misogynistic attack leads to his daughter Emily writing an article criticising Jeremy, her father, and for a week or so before Christmas both the Clarksons are in the news.

But, Christmas is a time for family, and Emily and her other sister Katya both return home. Jeremy says nothing about the articles and is grateful when his daughters don't bring it up. They spend a brilliant Christmas morning together and then Emily and Katya suggest it will be great to dress for dinner. Jeremy sighs good naturedly and puts on his tux, and he and Lisa, his girlfriend go downstairs. They sit at the table, curious to see what his daughters have in mind. Lisa is an ex model and of course wears something stunning.

But not as stunning as Emily and Katya. They walk in stark naked, each with a full chamber pot. They place them both on the table in front of Jeremy, and tell him to think of Meghan Markle.

How to End the Story

1. With Emily's last words.
2. Jeremy sheds a tear and apologises.
3. Jeremy refuses to apologise and instead goes on a rant about Megan Markle.

How to Start the Story

1. Insults from Jeremy's article
2. The rebuttal from Emily's article
3. The crisis of Emily and Katya arriving for Christmas and Jeremy waiting for them to refer to his article.
4. Jeremy's relief as he dresses into his tuxedo, thinking back over the articles and the great Christmas morning they've all shared.

These Boots Are Made for Talking

A teenager girl, Carla, is struggling to come out as gay to her divorced mother. She wants to, but is scared of the reaction. But she's also not comfortable being gay, she doesn't want everyone to know yet. She worries how people will react.

She goes Christmas shopping for clothes with her mother. They look at a blue pair of Doc Martens in the window. Carla likes them. Her mother Martina really likes them and suggests that her daughter ought to try them on. Carla refuses and comments that only a lesbian would be caught dead wearing them. Her mother laughs. As they walk down the street, they notice peoples shoes, and two girls walk by holding hands, each wearing a colourful pair of Doc Martens boots. Her mother christens them, Dyke Martins. They both laugh. Carla is furious with herself and her mother, but says nothing.

It's Christmas morning, and Carla is still unsure how to come out to her mother. She's filled with regret that she didn't take the chance to say something yesterday. She comes downstairs, willing herself to find her voice.

Her mother walks in. She is wearing bright blue Doc Martin boots. 'I think we need to talk,' she says.

How to Start the Story

1. Cara's thoughts, as he goes shopping with her mother.
2. The conversation about the boots, with Cara's thoughts and worries are revealed.

How to End the Story

1. Martina has bought them to help her Cara talk about being gay
2. Martina has bought them because she is bisexual, and is using them as a way to come out to Cara – this is partly hinted at earlier with the divorce

Be Careful What You Wish For

Stephen, a seven-year-old boy, watches the Apollo moon landings in 1969. He pesters his father, a carpenter, that he wants a rocket for Christmas. His parents always get him exactly what he wants for Christmas. He is a single child and they don't appear to know how to say no to him.

He keeps reminding his father that it can't just be a model rocket. It has to be big enough for him to fit inside it. It has to be a real rocket.

Stephen comes down on Christmas morning and finds an 8 foot rocket standing in his living room. He can't believe his eyes. It's so realistic, he's afraid that it might actually take off, but his father reassures him. He promises not to press the red ignition button in a box he holds in front of him.

Stephen steps into the rocket, and climbs into his padded chair. His father smiles at him and locks the latch. He begins a countdown from 30 seconds, as Stephen starts to beg his father, not to press the red button. As the count nears zero, he begins to scream. But his dad doesn't press the button, and Stephen sits back, relief flooding through his body.

He hears the front door slam. His parents have left. They don't come back till Boxing Day. You can imagine what those hours are like – the anger, terror and disappointment. But, eventually, Stephen is exhausted and falls asleep.

It's Boxing Day. The father opens the rocket to find his son sitting in soiled trousers. The sons eyes stare at him in disbelief.

His father smiles, and says, 'be careful what you wish for.'

How to Start the Story

1. A description of the Apollo landing
2. Stephen's demand for a rocket
3. Stephen's father, excited at finishing the perfect the Christmas present for his son – a present he knows his son will remember forever.

How to End the Story

1. I can't think of a better ending.
2. From Stephen's adult perspective – this is the best Christmas present he ever had
3. You don't have to end it cruelly – the father can open it up much earlier if you want to make it a magical Christmas

Past Present

A father has five kids. They're all grown up now between the ages of 19 and 32. They all resent him for the parts of their childhood where he went missing, or he remarried to horrible stepmothers while their real mother had died. Although it had not been his fault she died, it had been cancer, they all blamed him because he was not the mother that they wanted.

This Christmas, he listened to all their usual complaints and squabbles, and bought them each something completely inappropriate. The architect got a huge box of Lego. The journalist got a book on how to write. The doctor got a book on homeopathic medicine. The accountant got a book on Zen Buddhism. The house husband got a maids outfit. They all turn to him in puzzlement and disgust and humour mixed with anger. He smiled at them. I've given you the most precious gift of all, he said, shared memories. With that he chuckled and walked out to the pub.

He's dead now, and we all have children of our own, but sure enough we talk about it every Christmas. It has become a Christmas tradition where we will buy each other the most inappropriate present we can find.

How to Start the Story

1. The present, and the narrator is wrapping up something completely tasteless for one of her siblings. The story is told in flashback.
2. In the crisis – a sibling ranting to their father about the present they have just opened.
3. Focus on the father's smiling face as his children explode in all sorts of entertaining ways at the gifts he has given and the memories they bring to the surface.

How to End the Story

1. The narrator looking forward to another inappropriate gift giving.
2. The narrator opening their own inappropriate gift from a sibling, and telling the rest in flashback.

El Tigre

Brian is a backpacker on holiday in Mexico. He's young and broke and having a brilliant time. He sees a wrestler's mask of a tiger face and longs to buy it because it is glorious, over the top, and worn by his favourite wrestler, El Tigre. It is the kind with a zip at the back, and covers the whole head. But if he buys it, he can't pay the rent.

So instead he spends a year in Mexico, becomes fluent in Spanish and a great cook of Mexican food, but he leaves with only one regret. He never did buy that mask.

He returns home, builds a boring career in accounting, and gets engaged to Katerina. She's heard all about his time in Mexico and one birthday manages to track down one of Brian's Facebook friends with a sister in Tiahuanaco who knows the shop that sells the masks. She has it flown over from Mexico.

Brian is delighted. That first night, they joke around, and Katerina asks him to wear the mask in bed. They are both surprised and delighted at the change in his persona and his passion. But soon, Katerina will only allow him into the bedroom if he is wearing the mask. He feels wanted and rejected at the same time.

Soon she is pregnant. She has food cravings, like most mothers do. She develops an expensive urge to keep eating raw steak. They joke that the baby is going to be a massive boy.

How to End the Story

1. The baby's head emerges, already striped with black and gold hair.
2. The baby is born and when it takes its first breath, there is no newborn cry. Instead there is a growl.
3. As the baby is born, Katerina's voice changes from moans to a growl, and as she grips Brains arm, he is aware her fingers have grown claws.

How to Start the Story

1. With the first sighting of the mask in Tiahuanaco
2. When Brian opens his present of the mask.
3. In labour, with the rest told in flashback

The Fix

Aliyah is having fertility treatment, but it is not working. There are six courses, and the first five haven't worked. She knows she is ovulating today, and is due to take the last treatment. But she wonders if there is a better way? Instead of going to the fertility clinic, she decides to look up the poshest hotel she can find with a good gym, and finds one 80 miles away. She packs her best gym kit and heads off. She checks in and the concierge tells her the showers will be out of action for the next hour, but otherwise, first class service is guaranteed.

She changes and descends to the gym and pool, looking for attractive men, shopping in a gene pool. The price of the hotel maximises the chance that the men will be successful, hardworking and intelligent. Then there is height, proportion and symmetry to think about. What better place than the exclusive gym? Like Goldilocks, she sifts through the candidates as she trains, finding three who look the part. She engages all three in conversation – one is too arrogant, another is too vain, but the third has a sense of humour and is genuinely interested in talking to her, rather than scanning her lycra for curves.

She suggests a drink in the bar, and then she lays out her proposition. She is open about wanting to get pregnant, and this is going to be a one shot deal. He agrees, and she and Richard retire to her hotel room.

'I can fix your problem,' he says, 'and it will be my pleasure.'

Afterwards, he asks for her phone number and she gives him a false one. She's left her mobile at home in case her husband tracks it.

And that was that. Success. A baby girl, Amelia, is born. 12 months later, the boiler dies and her husband finds a plumber.

"I can fix that," says Richard, as Aliyah walks into the kitchen with Amelia in her arms.

How to End the Story

1. As it is, so we don't know if Richard is only talking about the plumbing
2. There is a spark of recognition from Amelia
3. Aliyah laughs, and the tension disappears
4. 'Crap,' thinks Aliyah, 'daddy is a plumber!'

How to Start the Story

1. 'Aliyah decided today was the day she would get pregnant'.
2. Or, start in media res, scanning suitable men in the gym.
3. Start with a crisis, the boiler dying, Aliyah looking at Amelia learning to walk, and remembering how she had been conceived. This happens in flashback before the plumber arrives.

The Most Famous Artist in the World

Jack had always known the future.

His mother visited a fortune teller, who predicted she would move to America, marry an unsuccessful actor, and have a son who becomes a famous artist.

And, Andrea would tell him, each birthday and Christmas, that this is how she came to Hollywood, this is how she married Arthur, one of the hardest working extras in Los Angeles, and why she had called him Jack, after the famous artist Jackson Pollock.

Over time, the family legend grew, and Jack was the great hope. With fame would come fortune, and the family would live, as the Americans say, high on the hog.

Jack threw himself into his artistic studies. His parents scrimped and saved to get him into the best schools. He became a master of colour, and experimented with new paints. He patented a glossy paint using hydrofluoric acid mixed with gold leaf. He could afford only one batch of paint, and used it for a dozen years. It produced vibrant and expensive masterpieces. But he didn't sell many. He earned just enough to keep him going. Fame and success just wouldn't come to him.

Then when Jack was 35, a famous film director (Quentin Tarantino) bought one of his paintings, full of blood reds and hints of violence. He knew this would lead to a flood of orders. And then it happened. Tarantino held an exhibition of his private collection. Jack and his parents were invited. The great and good of Hollywood were going to see one of his masterpieces, and they would be rich enough to afford his work. With a feeling of elation, dressed in their best clothes, Jack and his parents stood in front of his painting, drinking champagne with the rich and famous, with Hollywood royalty.

And this is how it happened. The hydrofluoric acid separated from the gold leaf. It burned a hole through each primary colour, and the canvas started to smoke in patches before his eyes. Within minutes, Tik Tok, YouTube and a dozen news channels were abuzz with his smoking painting. In houses around Los Angeles, canvases Jack had agonised over for the last dozen years, all began to smoke and turn black and grey with burnt-out holes.

And so it was that Jack became the most famous artist in the world.

How to Start the Story

1. At the art exhibition, Jack and his family elated.
2. One week later, Jack on a rooftop, wondering whether to jump – told in flashback
3. Jack, now famous and rich. His burnt out paintings have become cult classics. But his paintings are the complete opposite of what he values as art. Will he be bitter? Tell the story in flashback.

How to End the Story

1. Jack on the ledge, wondering whether to jump
2. Jack in mid-flight as he falls, his life passing before his eyes

3. Jack laughing his head off as he becomes rich
4. Jack laughing hysterically with Quentin Tarantino as he watches the painting smoulder
5. Jack giving up painting

Water into Wine

Eduardo was in love with Eugenie. She came from a wealthy family, and had a family name which stretched back through centuries of nobility. Eugenie's parents, Anne and Edward, were wealthy, but bored. Private helicopter, check. Private plane, check. Houses in London, Paris and Switzerland, check. Summers in Tuscany and Martha's Vineyard, check and check again.

Eugenie was a doctor, who wanted to make a difference in the world, rather than live off her parents' money. Eduardo worked for his family vineyard. Wine was his passion, second only, of course, to the beautiful Eugenie.

It would be Andrew's sixtieth birthday tomorrow, and Eugenie told Eduardo this would be the perfect time to ask for her parents' permission to marry her. All he had to do was impress them. But what do you get for parents who have more money than they know how to spend? Wine, said Eduardo, the most unusual wine that money can buy. Leave it to me, he told Eugenie.

In the month leading up to the birthday, Eduardo drank litres and litres of water every day. He sunbathed for an all over body tan. He shaved every hair from his body. At last he was ready, and told Eugenie the final part of his plan. She screamed in horror and delight. Then she said yes.

And so after the main course, Eduardo announced he had to get the desert wine, prepared especially in his parents' vineyard. He returned minutes later with the wine glasses, a silver tray, and a bottle as conspicuous by its absence as Eduardo's clothes. His tanned and sculpted body drew the eye, until he moved the tray to reveal all.

Eugenie spoke before her wide eyed parents could say anything. "Edo dear, pour me a wine, will you?" Edo drank a glass of water, then placed a wine glass between his legs and expressed a fragrant red wine, rich with hints of blackberry, one of the last examples of a 30 year old vintage.

"Surprise, daddy. The miracle of water into wine," she giggled, as Edo filled three more glasses, and handed them round the table.

How to End the Story

1. Eugenie empties the catheter* she had used to empty Eduardo's bladder, and fill it back up with wine.
2. Eduardo becomes an organiser of parties for the rich, climaxing in his signature service.
3. Edward and Anne welcome him into the family with open arms.

How to Start the Story

- Eduardo in training, drinking, tanning and shaving
- Eugenie telling Eduardo that he must impress her parents
- In media res - Eduardo, lying on his bed, while Eugenie expertly inserts a catheter.

- Eugenie in despair that her parents had everything, and couldn't be impressed by anything she could afford or do, or any man she could bring home to marry
- You could flip it, so that the idea is Eugenie's – we start in media res, as she gives an old man a catheter, and this gives her the idea.

*catheter – a flexible tube inserted into a narrow opening into a body cavity. (You can guess where). It is usually pushed into the bladder, to remove 'fluid'.

A Dog is not Just for Christmas

It's Christmas Eve. Princess, Fiona is the ugliest dog you ever saw. She is a balding potbellied Pitbull with chunks of fur missing and a waddling gait. One eye is much larger than the other and looks like it wasn't quite put on straight. She's missing two of her front teeth, so her tongue hangs out , pink, wet and smelling of last night's dog food. Every day at the dog shelter, she is trundled out for prospective owners who turn away in embarrassment or disgust.

One day five year old Miami arrives. Her mother, Houston is amused when Princess Fiona waddles up to Miami to lick her. Miami giggles with delight, throws her arms around Princess Fiona's neck and they both roll excitedly over the floor. The deal is done then and there and all the staff at the dog shelter form a line of honour and applaud the improbable departure of the ugliest dog they've ever seen.

Miami begs Houston to let Princess Fiona sleep on her bed. The magic of Christmas makes her mother relent. Princess Fiona flops gratefully onto the bed, drooling from one end and releasing gases from the other. Miami giggles excitedly and can barely sleep but Christmas works it's magic and she drifts off, excited about all that tomorrow will bring. Houston goes to sleep reflecting that this is the happiest her daughter has been.

While the people sleep, a strange pulse of energy enters the house. Princess Fiona begins to glow, her distended belly begins to shrink, her eyes align, large, and beautiful, her teeth grow back, and her fur develops a magnificent sheen.

She puts her head on Miami's pillow, so that she will be the first thing Miami's sees when she wakes. In the morning, Houston creeps in with Miami's stocking, and she is astonished to see the perfect dog, transformed on Miami's pillow. It's a Christmas miracle.

Miami opens her eyes and gazes at Princess Fiona with wide eyes.

How to End the Story

1. She screams and screams and screams. She is inconsolable. (My preferred ending!)
2. They take the dog back to the dog shelter in disgust.

How to Start the Story

1. With a description of Princess Fiona
2. With the viewpoint of Miami, meeting Princess Fiona
3. From Houston's perspective – so pleased to make her daughter happy with this bizarre dog.

Mary the Elephant

Elmo Gibbons became a human being half way through the first world war. In 1916 his circus, The Elmo Gibbons organised an elephant parade through Gloucester. Their star elephant was Mary, so intelligent she could play 29 tunes on car horns, and so skilful she could skate on ice.

Elmo hired some unemployed men, too old to go to war, to hold an elephant stick, a kind of spear, to prod each elephant if they didn't obey their rider. Now, Mary led the way, until she came to a small orchard of apple and pear trees. She had a sweet tooth, and stopped to eat. Nothing the rider could do would move her, and the crowds lining the route became impatient. The animals behind threatened to break ranks, and so Mary's minder prodded her jaw with the sharp end of his stick.

Mary was thrown into a rage, picked up her minder and threw him into the road. The crowd screamed and parted, only for Mary to roll him over and place one foot firmly on his head. The sounds of hundreds of people screaming brought the police and thousands of onlookers. Elmo watched it all in slow motion, his feelings moving from horror to delight. What a spectacle.

He announced that for only one shilling, tonight's show would be an execution. The first and only public hanging of an elephant.

That night, town was full. It was the largest profit Elmo ever made. A crane stood in the town square, dangling a huge chain. The chain was looped around Mary's neck. Elmo looked into her eyes, and could tell she knew what was coming. Still, he ordered the crane driver to lift Mary, kicking as she rose. Elmo the showman was giving the public what they wanted, condemning Mary for her murderous crime, when the chain snapped, and Mary crashed downwards. Elmo dived in time to save his life, but Mary's hip crashed onto his legs, crushing them to a pulp. Elmo would never forget the pain nor Mary's screams.

Still, the show must go on. Mary, her pelvis shattered, was hanged at the second attempt. Elmo would never walk again. But the doctor who treated him at the scene also examined Mary. She had an abscess the size of a football in her jaw, exactly where the minder had prodded her.

And that's when, in 1916, the Mary Gibbons circus became the first circus in the world without animals.

How to Start the Story

1. In the crisis, with the screaming
2. With a portrait of Mary, the amazingly intelligent elephant, playing her tunes
3. With a portrait of Mary waiting to be hung, with flashback
4. Elmo's narration, telling his story to his children – what did you do during the war daddy?

How to End the Story

1. Elmo, as a reformed man, like Ebenezer Scrooge
2. Elmo, reliving his and Mary's screams
3. A circular structure, a memory of Mary playing a tune which plays now on the gramophone

Nine Lives

Dolly makes a parachute jump. She's 28 years old. It's 1912, and in those days you held tight and let the wind take you. This is told in flashback, as she falls to earth, and gradually notices that she is heading towards a railway track.

Dolly has risked her life every week since she was 16. At 16, she took a job as a waitress at Alexandra Palace, so she could hear her favourite band. One of her customers was Buffalo Bill, and he encouraged her to volunteer to be the girl standing with objects on her head, while he, the blindfolded sharp shooter, would shoot them.

Then came the trapeze act – not messing about with a circus, but on a hot air balloon, before parachuting back to earth. Another death was cheated when, at 15,000 ft the altitude made breathing difficult, and it was a toss up whether the cold would kill her before suffocation. She had managed climb up the ropes and let out some helium, to get the balloon down.

Then there was a duo act with Mary, who's parachute didn't open, so she clung onto Dolly all the way down. They landed with so much force that Dolly was paralysed. The doctors decided to electrocute her legs gently to stimulate them. One doctor miscalculated the charge. It flew her off the bed in spasms and knocked her unconscious. But the fall miraculously realigned her spine. Dolly made a full recovery and decided to get straight back up in the balloon.

This is a dozen jumps later. It is her 100th jump, and she now notices that a train is going to meet her as she falls towards the tracks. She can veer left or right, but doing that will only plunge her into trees whose branches will break her limbs and crush her skull. There seems no way she can cheat death.

And then the train driver spots her. He knows exactly what to do. He watches her fall to exactly the right spot and lets out a giant column of steam. It throws her over the tree tops and she lands a few hundred meters away in the Grantham canal.

She can't swim, of course. But is astonished to find that it is only 5 foot deep. This is when she decided to retire!

How to Start the Story

1. From Dolly's point of view, at the beginning of the last jump – perfect weather and views, to contrast with all the times she has cheated death, in flashback.
2. From Dolly's daughter, Molly's, point of view, looking back and imagining the life of her mother on the occasion of her 86th birthday, when she is making one last jump with the Red Devils.

How to End the Story

1. In the canal.
2. She finds out who the train driver was, and propositions him – they get married.

3. Just before she lands in the canal, observing to herself that this is another fine mess – if only she had learned to swim. We have to decide if she survives.

Heroes

It is 1915. Rex Warneford is a 24 year old flying ace in the First World War.

The story is told by a British journalist. Rex has refused to take him up in a plane. It is a new plane, which Rex is delivering to the naval airbase. He has decided to take an American journalist, Henry Beach Needham, instead, because he wants to be internationally famous. "I need him," he says, as a pun.

He has just received a medal, the Légion d'honneur from the French Army Commander in Chief, General Joffre, because he single-handedly downed a German Zeppelin airship on its way to bomb England. He managed to avoid its machine guns, climb above it and drop six bombs on it. It crashed on a convent school, killing some schoolgirls and couple of nuns. The explosion spun his plane out of control and he crash-landed behind German lines. He still managed to repair his plane just before he was captured, yelling to the Germans "Give my regards to the Kaiser!"

He has already received the Victoria Cross for this (the collateral damage was ignored).

Rex is really called Reginald, but Rex means king in Latin, and he prefers this as a nickname. Rex fancies himself. He is drunk from the celebration and meal with General Joffre, and insults the British journalist.

And so, he takes up the American in the new plane, and at 200 feet, the right wings just snap right off. They plummet to the ground, and both men are killed.

The British journalist writes a brilliant article, portraying the tragic death of the hero.

The best tribute is in his home town. In an ironic twist they open a new school and name it after him, Warneford School.

How to Start the Story

1. At the crisis point, evading machine gun fire and bombing the zeppelin.
2. Mid argument with the British journalist, refusing to take him in the plane.
3. At the crisis point, where the wings sheer off, reported by the watching British journalist.

How to End the Story

1. With the ironic naming of the school
2. With his death
3. With the wings sheering off, and his realisation that there is no escape from death

A Close Shave

There were gods of the wind, and gods of the sun and moon, gods of the harvest and gods of the stars. Fertility gods, and gods of fate. 100 gods, one for each of Avebury's 100 stones.

The pagan gods were furious. Christians in Avebury in 1350 were busy attacking the stone circle, praying to their god and cursing the old gods, the old ways, the generations who had lived here for thousands of years, and the gods who had prospered for thousands of years, long before Jesus.

The villagers were digging at the stone's bases. 12 stones to represent the 12 disciples. The Christians prayed and sang and feasted and dug.

By far the loudest was the travelling barber. He sang with the loudest voice. He spoke most persuasively as he cut the wives' hair, softly pointing out the sacrilege of the stones surrounding the church. He spoke loudest to the men as he trimmed their beards, painting the pagans as dangerous enemies, and the stones as obstacles to good farming and the plough.

The barber had arrived on the first of January, and it had taken till Easter to work the village into a frenzy of zeal and action. The day that Jesus rose would be the day that the stones fell. The day that the stone was rolled from Christ's tomb so that he rose again would be the day the stones were toppled and buried in Avebury.

The barber hacked at the trickster God's stone – the Vikings called him Loki, and before them the Celts called him Lugh, but his real name was lost in time. He drank his wine and laughed while the barber led the digging, deeper and deeper, while the congregation pushed the stone back and forth, like loosening a giant tooth. And then the barber made the final cut, his pick axe dislodging a stone at the base, and the giant stone began to fall. The barber ran for edge of his hole, and scrabbled at the sides. He would look back on this as a close shave. But the scissors in his pocket stabbed him in the side. No harm done, really. An inch of stabbing, painful but survivable. But just enough to make him cry out and pause. And he looked back, as the stone fell on him, crushing him down into the earth.

900 years later the archaeologists raised the stones and placed his body in the British Museum.

How to Start the Story

1. In media res, with the pagan gods arguing
2. In flashback, with the barber, persuading customers to attack the stones
3. With (make up a name), the god of mischief looking at the barber's skeleton in the British museum, telling the story in flashback
4. A visitor to Avebury presses their hands on the stone in a storm/ at dawn/ on the solstice/ and has a sudden vision of what happened
5. The barber, watching the stone fall, and his past flashing before his mind's eye

How to End the Story

1. The barber, as a cautionary tale or pathetic figure displayed in the British Museum
2. The god of mischief watching the stone crush the barber
3. The barber's perspective, as the stone falls
4. The archaeologist carefully uncovers the barber's scissors or skull, or perhaps his hand crushed against his skull, revealing he had tried to ward off the falling stone.

Eilmer the Flying Monk

Eilmer was a monk and a dreamer. He knew his classic myths, and he believed Daedalus might actually have flown. He didn't believe in wings made of wax. But he thought silk might work. He built wings which stretched from his wrists to his ankles. The other monks humoured him. Eilmer was always inventing something. His greenhouse was like the Garden of Eden. But flying? Dream on Eilmer.

'There will be a sign from God,' said Eilmer. And sure enough, there was. A comet, Halley's comet, streaked across the sky with a blazing tail.

And so, Eilmer put on his suit of silk. His wings stretched from his wrists to his ankles. He looked more like a bat than an angel. He gave a rousing speech and the Abbot prayed for him. Then, all the monks gathered beneath Malmesbury Abbey's tallest tower. They kissed him. They commended his soul to heaven. They lifted up their eyes.

Eilmer jumped. Or rather he launched. He sprang forward and spread his arms and legs. He jumped from the tower of the abbey, and streaked like a comet.

But then, instead of gliding smoothly, he began to spin. He flapped, and flailed, and righted himself, and spun again. Yet he flew 200 meters before spinning and crash-landing in a field.

He broke both his legs, and though the right one healed well, the left was never straight. He walked with a stick and a limp. But this was a small sacrifice to be the first man to fly and live. He was a miracle.

He knew he had been lucky. Because the sign of God, the blazing comet, well, that had had a tail. He understood that, like every bird, all he had needed was a tail. He could fly better next time. But his brother monks knew that one miracle was enough.

One by one, the other monks died off, replaced by new men, who treated Eilmer's flight as a legend, or a myth. But he did live to see Halley's comet return 75 years later in 1066. Some say he put on his silk flying suit once more, with a new tail stretched over a frame of cane. And, they say, he flew once more from the top of the tower.

And that, so they say, was the last anyone ever saw of Eilmer.

How to Start the Story

1. The voice of God, telling Eilmer he can fly.
2. Or flashback, Eilmer's voice as he tells of his first attempt, 75 years ago.
3. Or a witness to the final flight, where Eilmer vanishes, telling the story for future generations.
4. With prayers from the monks as they watch Eilmer prepare for his leap.

How to End the Story

1. Eilmer disappears in flight
2. Eilmer thanking God for his broken legs

3. Eilmer, aged 93, standing on top of the tower, ready to jump with his new suit and tail.

Printed in Great Britain
by Amazon

32467896R00020